I Love Sports
Soccer

by Allan Morey

Bullfrog Books

Ideas for Parents and Teachers

Bullfrog Books let children practice reading informational text at the earliest reading levels. Repetition, familiar words, and photo labels support early readers.

Before Reading

- Discuss the cover photo. What does it tell them?

- Look at the picture glossary together. Read and discuss the words.

Read the Book

- "Walk" through the book and look at the photos. Let the child ask questions. Point out the photo labels.

- Read the book to the child, or have him or her read independently.

After Reading

- Prompt the child to think more. Ask: Have you played soccer before? Have you watched a game? What did each player do?

Bullfrog Books are published by Jump!
5357 Penn Avenue South
Minneapolis, MN 55419
www.jumplibrary.com

Library of Congress Cataloging-in-Publication Data

Morey, Allan.
  Soccer / by Allan Morey.
     pages cm. — (I love sports)
  Summary: "This photo-illustrated book for early readers introduces the basics of soccer and encourages kids to try it. Includes labeled diagram of soccer field and photo glossary." — Provided by publisher.
  Includes index.
  Audience: Age: 5.
  Audience: Grade: K to Grade 3.
  ISBN 978-1-62031-181-3 (hardcover) —
  ISBN 978-1-62496-268-4 (ebook)
  1. Soccer for children—Juvenile literature.
I. Title.
  GV944.2.H64 2015
  796.334—dc23
                                                   2014032130

Series Editor: Rebecca Glaser
Series Designer: Ellen Huber
Book Designer: Anna Peterson
Photo Researcher: Jenny Fretland VanVoorst

Photo Credits: All photos by Shutterstock except: Corbis, 5; iStock, 8–9, 19, 23mr, 23br; Thinkstock, 3, 4, 6–7, 12–13, 14–15, 20–21, 23ml, 23bl, 24.

Printed in the United States of America at Corporate Graphics in North Mankato, Minnesota.

Table of Contents

Let's Play Soccer!

Grab a ball.

Put on your cleats.

Let's play soccer!

Ava's team gets the ball first.

She dribbles the ball with her feet.

She does not use her hands.

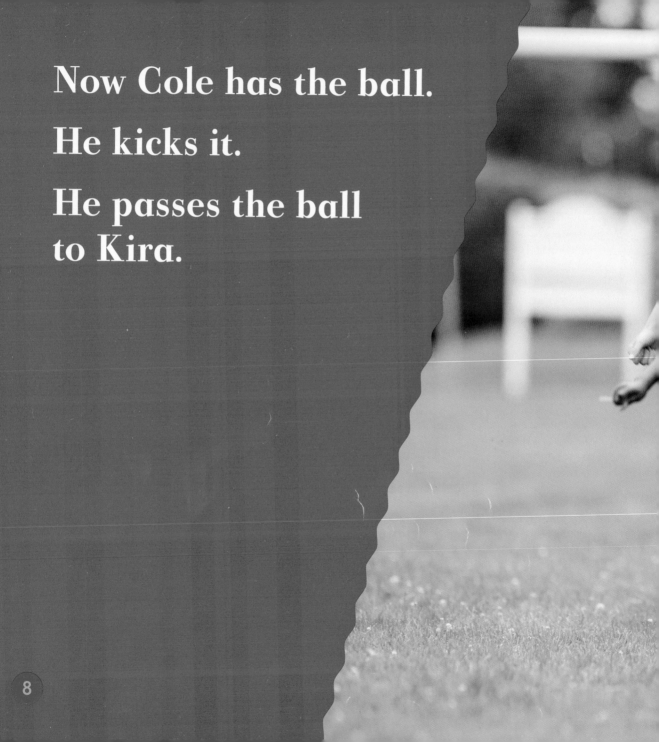

Now Cole has the ball.

He kicks it.

He passes the ball
to Kira.

pass

Jen jumps.

She heads the ball.

The ball flies at the goal.

Brad is the goalie.
He grabs the ball.
He stops it from
going into the goal.

Now Will's team
has the ball.

He passes it down
the field.

John gets the ball.

He kicks it to the goal.

The goalie dives.

The ball flies into the net.
Goal!

Now John's team
is ahead by one.

Do you want to play?

Kick a ball.

Soccer is fun!

At the Soccer Field

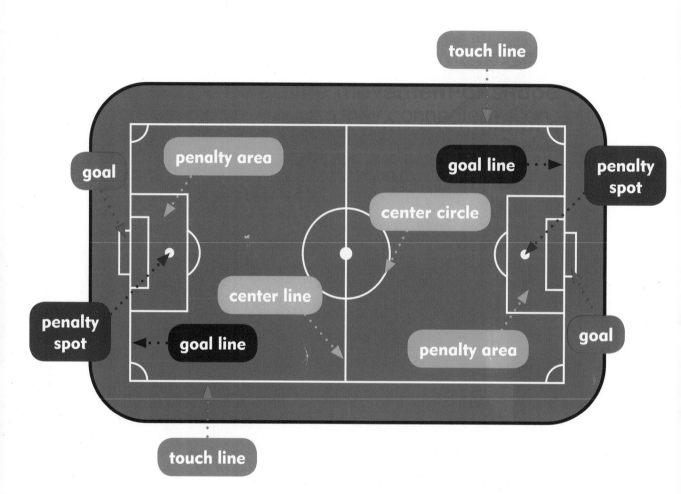

Picture Glossary

cleats
Shoes with spikes on the bottom to help keep players from slipping on grassy fields.

head
In soccer, to hit the ball with your forehead.

dribble
To move the ball down the field with short, light kicks.

pass
To move the ball down the field by kicking it to a teammate.

goalie
The player who stands in front of the net to block the other team from scoring.

team
A group of players who play together; there are 11 players on a soccer team.

Index

To Learn More

Learning more is as easy as 1, 2, 3.

1) Go to www.factsurfer.com

2) Enter "soccer" into the search box.

3) Click the "Surf" button to see a list of websites.

With factsurfer.com, finding more information is just a click away.